Degutopia

GW01466216

Degu Care

Dr. Chloe Long

This book was created as a companion to the information contained on Degutopia's website.

Degutopia

~Dedicated to the health and well-being of degus everywhere~

To find out more, visit

http://www.degutopia.co.uk

ISBN-13: 978-1503054660

About the Author

Dr. Chloe Long is the founder of and main contributor to Degutopia, an information service dedicated to promoting the health and well-being of degus around the world. Chloe obtained her PhD in Bioacoustics from Loughborough University in the UK. She is widely published in the behaviour, vocalisations and biology of both degus and bats, and has a lifelong passion for animals and science. Chloe discovered and fell in love with her first degu in 2002, created the Degutopia website in 2004, and hasn't looked back since! Her goal in this book is to make high-quality scientific information available to degu owners in an easily understandable form.

The author wishes to thank Jim Hague and Melissa Tiley-Waters for their assistance.

This book is dedicated to Jeremy, the original Degutopia degu.

Contents

An Introduction to Degus

Degus have evolved in a very specific part of the world- in the wild they are only found in Chile, South America! The degu is a unique type of rodent belonging to the caviomorph family; their closest relatives are the guinea pig and the chinchilla, which also come from this part of the world. In central Chile, degus live between the Pacific coast and the Andes mountains. Unlike chinchillas, degus aren't able to live at high altitudes and prefer to live around sea level where the climate is warmer. Because degus live in such a specific area, they have special adaptations to allow them to live in a

Map of South America showing the wild degu distribution in Chile (red).

semi-arid environment. One such adaptation is their ability to conserve water, which is particularly important in hot and dry conditions. Degus therefore do not sweat, but rely instead on the flow of blood to their ears, much as elephants do, to keep cool. They also produce concentrated urine and even have special cells in their nasal passages to help prevent water loss through

Degus are adapted to the high-fibre diet of a semi-arid scrubland.

breathing. Because the Chilean climate is so dry for many months of the year, this has resulted in another special adaptation in the degu, relating to their diet. Long, dry summers mean many plants find it difficult to grow in the degus' habitat, and their most important food resources, herbs and grasses, are dried and very fibrous for much of the year. To cope with eating this dry, fibrous food, all degu teeth grow continuously in order to combat the regular wear they receive. You'll be reading more about how importantly this affects your pet degus' diet later on.

Wild degus also construct and use series of burrows that they call home. These are used for sleeping, storing food, hiding from predators and rearing pups. These underground burrows are also really important for keeping cool in hot weather (and for huddling in to keep warm in the cold!). Degus are often termed 'semi-fossorial' because they use their burrows for some of the day, but also spend a lot of time foraging for food above ground. Degus are also diurnal, meaning 'active during the day', in contrast with chinchillas which are nocturnal and active at night. However, degu activity does vary according to the season, and in the summer, wild degus will only spend mornings and evenings out and about foraging for food, spending the hottest part of the day sleeping underground where it's cooler. Having a siesta is a great way to conserve energy, particularly when mid-day summer temperatures in Chile can reach over 40 °C!

Degus are highly social animals and thrive in a group environment. Wild degu colonies typically consist of groups of around 6 breeding females and 1-2 males, or smaller groups of 'bachelor' males. Because they are naturally preyed upon in the wild by animals like the Culpeo fox and black-chested buzzard, being in a group is particularly important to degus so that group members can take turns to watch for predators (safety in numbers!). It also allows degus to work together to complete tasks that use a lot of energy, such as digging burrows- researchers have observed wild degus forming digging 'chains' to excavate their tunnels!

Degus are naturally social animals.

Some cool facts about degus!

* Degus can see in *two colours*- green and ultraviolet (UV)! Humans can't see UV light, so the world must look very different to them.

* Degus have *UV reflective belly fur*! This allows them to signal to each other when they are watching for predators.

* On average, captive degus live for 6-8 years, which is roughly *three times longer* than a rat (2-3 years), *five times longer* than a dwarf hamster (1-2 years) and *2,190 times longer* than a mayfly (1 day)!

* Degus *use a wide variety of vocal sounds* to communicate, most of which are audible to humans. They also have a good hearing range and can respond to the human voice!

Check out the following related pages on Degutopia's website:

* Where do degus come from?
  * http://www.degutopia.co.uk/deguorigin.htm
* The wild degu lifestyle:
  * http://www.degutopia.co.uk/degulife.htm
* The wild degu community:
  * http://www.degutopia.co.uk/degucomm.htm
* The habitat of the wild degu:
  * http://www.degutopia.co.uk/deguhab.htm

Appearance of the Degu

Degus have a unique appearance that is full of character. Some of a degu's most distinctive features include kidney-shaped ears, a long, tufted tail covered with fine black bristles, circles of light fur around each eye, and bright orange teeth!

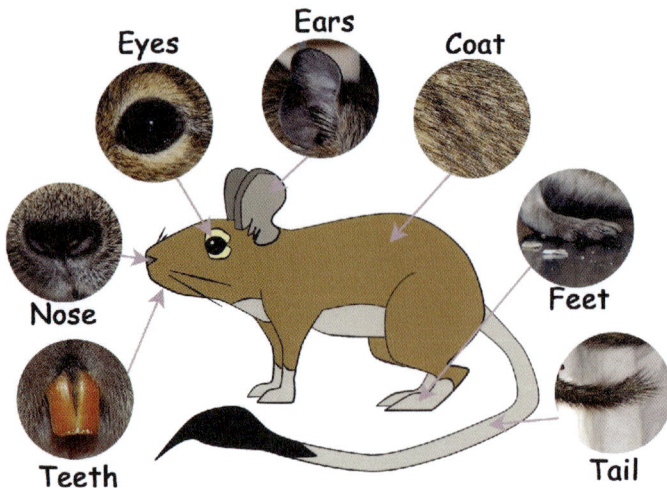

Eyes

Ears

Coat

Nose

Feet

Teeth

Tail

Teeth

Although degus have a total of 20 teeth, most of these are molar teeth used for grinding up food inside the mouth, and these are very hard to see without examining the mouth cavity. The most visible teeth are the incisors, two pairs of teeth at the front of the degu's mouth. In a healthy degu the incisor teeth should be even in length and show enamel of a bright orange colour- we'll talk more about teeth colour and shape in the health chapter.

Nose

Degu noses are hairless and have a dark pigmentation, complete with two narrow nostrils. The nose is an important piece of sensory equipment, as degus are able to obtain a lot of information from different smells (much more than humans can!). They can even detect little packets of chemical information called 'pheromones', which they use to identify the age, sex and physical condition of other degus in the area. Whiskers, found to the left and right of the nose, are also extremely important to the degu as they allow them to investigate the size and shape of an object, or a space. This is particularly handy for assessing whether a tunnel or gap is

'Whisking' objects while smelling them allows the degu to extract more information on size and shape than scent alone.

large enough for them to squeeze into without getting stuck! The nose is also essential to a degu because they are nasal breathers and aren't able to breathe normally through their mouths.

Eyes

Although degu eyes appear completely black in colour, in actual fact it is only the pupil in the centre that is black, while the iris surrounding it is a dark brown colour; this can be seen more easily when your degu is sitting near a good light source, such as near a window. Degus generally have good vision, although they can't see well in the dark. They do, however, rely a lot on other senses, such as hearing and smell. Checking the eyes is also important for assessing

In good light you'll notice that the degu iris is dark brown rather than black.

health, which again we'll be looking at later, in the health chapter.

Ears

Similar to the nose, degu ears are also pigmented but are covered with small, fine hairs. There are some much larger, bristly 'guard hairs' over the entrance to the ear canal; these are to help prevent debris from entering the ear canal (particularly important during dust-bathing!). Because degus rely on their ears for keeping cool in hot weather you might also notice changes to how your degu's ears look during the day; when they're feeling warm, degus stick up their ears which become pink. This is due to increased blood circulation to the ears, helping them lose bodyheat. A cold degu will have much paler ears, holding them folded down closer to their head, which helps to prevent heat loss through them. Degus also have sensitive hearing and sudden or unusual noises can make them run and hide, during which they give an alarm call to warn other degus of possible danger.

Coat

The normal coat colouration of a degu is a sandy brown colour, which is called 'agouti'. This is a special term given to hairs in the coat that, instead of being one solid colour, have bands of two or more colours. Hairs in the coats of degus are banded in light brown and grey. In the wild, this colouration camouflages degus against the sandy soil of their natural habitat. While agouti is still the most common colour for degu coats in captivity, other colours are also being developed, such

Degus have banded agouti hairs.

as 'blue', 'champagne agouti' and 'white patched agouti'. However, the health and genetics of these different varieties is often not as good, due to the inbreeding used to initially obtain some of them. Degus moult their entire coats around twice per year, their main shed is in the spring when they replace their long, thicker winter coats for a shorter, lighter summer coat.

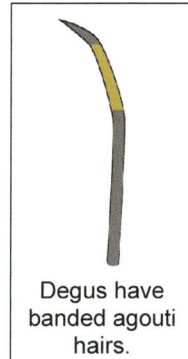

Feet

Although degus walk on all four feet, their front legs and forepaws are much smaller than their hind legs, being used mostly for grasping food while they eat and for manipulating objects. Their hind limbs are much more powerful and allow the degu to run at speed (up to 5 metres per second- that's as fast as your average cyclist!) and to jump reasonably high.

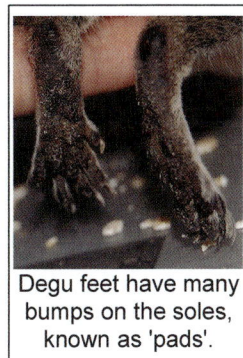

Degu feet have many bumps on the soles, known as 'pads'.

The soles of all four paws are covered with tough skin and also many small, knobbly bumps which are the 'pads'. These pads of spongy, fatty tissue act like cushions to protect the joints in the feet, much like the pads on a dog's or cat's paw do.

Degus mostly use their forepaws for grasping food while eating.

Tail

Degu tails are covered with bristly, black hairs that become longer toward the tip, forming a 'brush'. Degu tails are used for communication (both visual and audible by beating the tail on the floor) and also for balance while running, jumping and climbing. Their tails also have one other vital function- in the wild they're used to escape predators! This is because the degu tail can be detached, a process also known as 'de-gloving', allowing a degu

Degu tails end in a small 'brush' of black hairs.

caught by the tail to escape. For this reason it's important never to grab or hold a degu by the tail- a shed tail will never grow back! We'll talk more about handling and de-gloving later.

Determining the Sex of a Degu

There is little difference in appearance, size, behaviour or personality between male and female degus. Nonetheless, determining the sex of your degus isn't too difficult, once you know what to look for! The area that will show you their gender is called the anogenital region, which can be seen by gently lifting the base of the tail upwards while the degu is standing on a flat surface. Remember that you must not restrain a degu by their tail, but you can occupy them with a tasty pile of porridge oats to eat while you lift their tail! The two features to identify are the 'cone' and the 'anus'. In both sexes, the anus is always closest to the tail; this is where droppings are excreted from the body. Both sexes also have a 'cone', which is a pointy bit of skin in front of the anus, through which urination occurs.

Here is what you will see when you lift the tail:

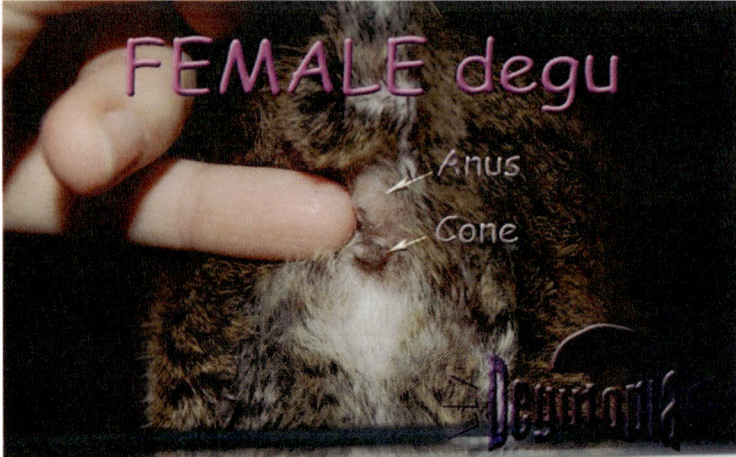

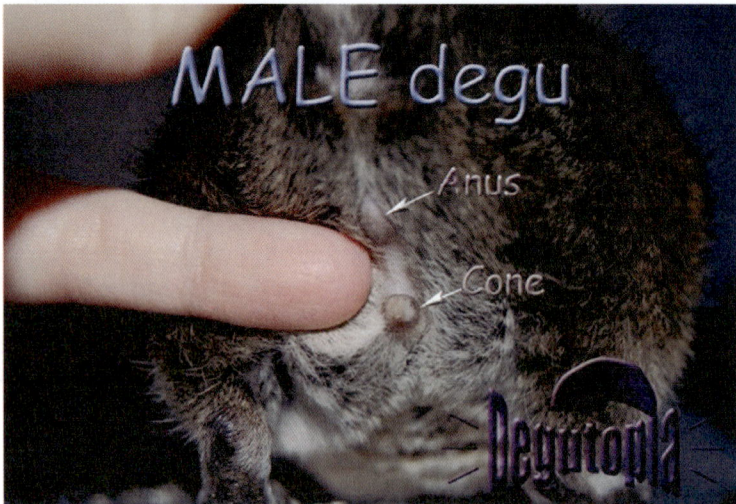

The difference between the two pictures above is the distance between the cone and the anus. In the male degu, there is a clear gap between the two (approximately the width of your little finger), whereas in females there is almost no gap at all. This is a good way to tell which sex your degus are, by remembering that:

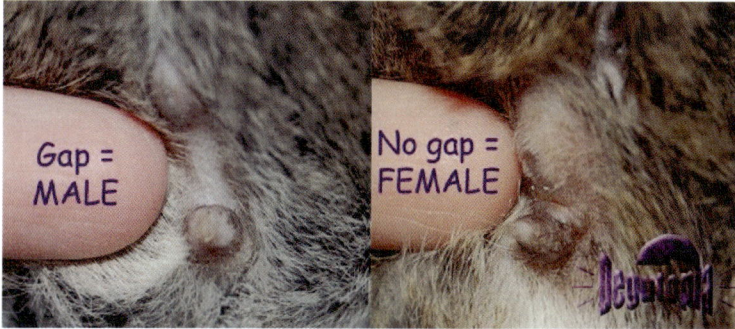

It's worth noting here that degus of any age can be accurately sexed using this same method; you can even determine the sex of a pup just a few minutes old this way! Below are some examples of pups aged 4 weeks old. Everything is a little smaller, but the 'gap rule' still applies!

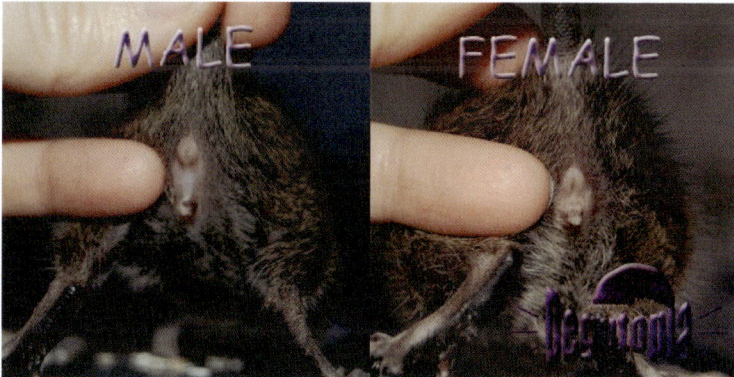

Check out the following related pages on Degutopia's website:

≥ Degu appearance and biology:
> ≥ http://www.degutopia.co.uk/deguapps.htm

≥ Video guide to sexing degus:
> ≥ http://www.degutopia.co.uk/degusexing.htm

≥ Degu colour varieties:
> ≥ http://www.degutopia.co.uk/degucolours.htm

Degu Housing

Any new degu owner will at some point need to make a decision on the type of housing needed for their degus. As with any addition to the degus' environment, the best starting point is to look at how degus live in the wild, so that you can best choose things that will meet their needs appropriately.

The very first thing you'll need to decide is: *How many degus should I get?*

As mentioned in the introduction, wild degus live in groups and have evolved to be highly social animals. For this reason, it is **really important** that you don't keep a degu on their own whenever you have the choice. Singly housed degus require a lot of attention from their human owners as a 'substitute group', and easily become depressed and even physically ill if they don't get the attention they need. **Always** try to keep at least a pair of degus together, and make sure they are the same sex (males will live in groups just as happily as females!).

Degus should be housed in social groups of the same sex, like these males.

Should I get male or female degus?

This choice is really up to you. Because there is little difference in appearance, behaviour or personality between male and female degus, it doesn't really matter. A male and female degu should not be housed together as they will breed (even if directly related); breeding is **not** recommended for the first-time owner!

The next important thing to address is the size of enclosure you plan to keep your degus in- this will also affect how many degus you should have, as each degu you keep will require enough space to be happy and perform a full range of normal behaviours. Degus are active animals and require plenty of space in their enclosure to get the exercise they need each day. The recommended **minimum size** of enclosure for housing a pair of adult degus is:

Length 70 x Width 45 x Height 100 cm

This will provide your degus with an internal volume of space appropriate for their needs. If you're planning on keeping more than two degus, it's a good idea to check that your enclosure has enough room for more degus. A good way to do that is to use the free 'cage space calculator' available on the housing page of Degutopia's website to check the dimensions (the link can be found at the end of the chapter). Bear in mind that your degu will need regular exercise and play times in a suitable space outside the cage, either in a degu-proofed room (all wires, houseplants and chewables removed!) or a large play pen. This is also very important for them to allow

Getting the size of your degu enclosure right is vital to their well-being.

the running, jumping and climbing exercise they may not be able to get inside the cage, as well as providing them with important mental stimulation through exploring and interacting with you. It's recommended that degus be let out for play times every day for at least half an hour.

What type of enclosure should I get for my degu?

There are many different types of enclosure available to house your degu comfortably. The enclosure will be the single largest expense of keeping degus, but it should last them their whole life. Degus appreciate extra height in enclosures rather than length, as they like to sit at the top to watch the world go by! If you have a choice therefore, go for a taller cage rather than a wide one, adding plenty of shelves, branches and hammocks. The most popular enclosures are as follows:

Degu/Chinchilla Cages

These are by far the most popular and suitable type of enclosure, and often the most affordable. Usually built mainly from steel or galvanized mesh, these cages often have deep bases to best contain the substrate that degus like to dig in. Shelves are normally made from kiln dried pine.

✓ Pro's	✗ Con's
• Well ventilated • Deep bases • Solid shelves • All-metal construction • Long-lasting	• Door openings can be small/restrictive • Can sometimes have a fixed mesh floor

Rat Cages

Also commonly available are the types of cage used to house rats. These are also made mainly of metal mesh that has been powder coated with enamel to protect it. These cages typically have more level divisions in them which are often made of mesh and may be removable, to be replaced with branches and hammocks for degu use.

✔️ Pro's	❌ Con's
• Well ventilated • Deep bases • All-metal construction	• Door openings can be small/restrictive • Can sometimes have a plastic base • Powder coating may wear off leading to rusting • Mesh levels and shelves need to be covered/removed

Bird/Parrot Cages

Image: Sarah Hudson

Bird cages can be a little more expensive, but are usually much bigger than other cage types. They are typically made from strong steel bars rather than mesh but usually lack any shelves or platforms- these can be added later or improvised with branches and hammocks.

✔️ Pro's	❌ Con's
• Well ventilated • Long-lasting • Lots of space	• Usually have plastic bases that need covering/replacing • Shelves need to be added • Bases may be shallow and don't hold substrate well • Bar spacing must be checked (not too wide)!

Ferret Cages

Usually a lot bigger than standard degu or rat cages but offering additional platforms and levels. These are typically made from a sturdy steel construction of bars rather than mesh. The bases are often deep, but watch out for plastic bases and plastic shelves!

✔ Pro's	✘ Con's
• Well ventilated • Long-lasting • Lots of space • Usually have big doors for good access • Usually have deep bases	• Can have plastic bases and/or shelves that need covering/replacing • Bar spacing must be checked (not too wide)!

Vivariums with Tank Toppers

Image: Kristine Couture

Vivariums and aquariums are popular for housing some small pets, such as gerbils. However, these are only suitable for housing degus when a tank topper is added (a mesh cage 'hat'), to increase space, provide extra height and improve ventilation.

✔️ Pro's	❌ Con's
• Extra deep base to contain substrate • Extra height for climbing	• Can be on the small side • Tank topper may need to be custom made • Can be heavy to lift for cleaning

Some important things to remember when choosing your degu enclosure:

1. Mesh bases- These are not suitable for degus, as they are prone to a condition known as 'pododermatitis' (also called 'bumblefoot'). This results in pressure sores/ulcers developing on the pads of the degu's feet if they have to walk on mesh or uneven surfaces regularly. Degus therefore *must* have a smooth base and shelves in their cage, or the mesh should be covered over, for example with ceramic tiles. Many cages have a removable mesh base, so do check before you buy that it doesn't have to be used!

2. Plastic bases- Degus are chewers, they need to chew or gnaw regularly to keep their incisor teeth short. For this reason, they can make short work of plastic based cages and escape! If you're buying a cage with a plastic base, remember to check that the base can be replaced with something more appropriate, or that it is safely contained within the cage. It's still a good idea to replace plastic bases with metal ones wherever possible- the manufacturer may even be able to supply one.

3. Bar spacing- This is particularly important to check before you buy, as if the bar spacing is too wide your degus won't hang around inside for long! Even adult degus can squeeze through any bar spacing wider than 2 cm, so be sure that the spacing is **less than 2 cm**.

4. Total cage size- Remember to be *absolutely sure* that the cage size you're buying is really suitable for the number of degus you're getting, it's *really important*! Purchasing a cage can be costly, so finding that your degus aren't happy living inside it could be an expensive mistake! If in doubt, **always double check the dimensions**. It is advised to go for the largest cage you can afford or can fit into your home- the bigger the cage the better for your degus' welfare.

Enclosure Enrichment

The next important task is to furnish and enrich your degus' cage appropriately. There are several key items that all degus need inside the cage to live comfortably, as follows:

Running wheel

This is first on the list because it's so important for your degus! The use of a running wheel has been shown to be a substitute for foraging behaviour, which degus spend a lot of time doing in the wild. Degus can run up to 4.5 kilometres per day- that's like running the length of Loch Ossian in Scotland! The wheel must be solid, having no rungs or spokes to trap legs and tails. Metal wheels are preferable to plastic as they aren't chewable and last far longer, but these can be tricky to find. Most important is the size of the wheel- it must be **at least 12 inches** in diameter. Wheels smaller than this cause the degu's

Wheels are an essential addition to your degu enclosure.

Degus can even learn to use 'flying saucer'-type wheels!

back to be arched while running, which can damage their spine.

Hay rack

Another essential is a place to store hay, keeping it off the floor, clean and tasty. As you'll read later, hay is a vital part of the degu diet, something which they need to browse on throughout the day. A hay rack will work well, as do mesh 'hay cubes' hung inside the cage. Degus also use hay to build their nests, along with other materials.

Nest box

Because degus use underground burrows for sleeping in the wild, having something that simulates this in the cage

A place to nest and hide away will make your degu feel right at home.

is important. A nest box or small space your degu can hide away and snuggle in is ideal for this. You can buy chinchilla nesting boxes made from kiln dried pine, or you can use a cardboard box (though it will need replacing from time to time). A big hit with degus is a hanging, enclosed hammock for sleeping in! Nests can be lined with strips of soft kitchen paper, shredded paper and hay. Avoid using cotton-based fluffy bedding as this can get wrapped around legs and tails.

Dust bath

You may not want to keep this inside the cage all the time, or have it just in the degu play area, but a dust bath is necessary for your degu to use regularly. Dust bathing is not only important for maintaining a healthy, grease-free coat, but it is also a behavioural necessity. Degus are born with the innate ability to dust bathe, but do need to learn the right place in which to do it! A shallow bowl full of chinchilla dusting clay is ideal- but be prepared for dust to fly out from all sides! Enclosed bath houses are available as a tidier option.

Food bowls and drinking bottles

Maintaining good food and water hygiene is critical to health. Food dishes are essential to hold your degus' daily hard feed portion while they eat- but don't forget to get one for each degu to avoid meal-time squabbles! It's also not a good idea to provide water in an open dish as this can get dirty quite quickly- it's better to use a drinking bottle. Those suitable for chinchillas and rabbits are ideal, either the ball-bearing type or the lever operated ones.

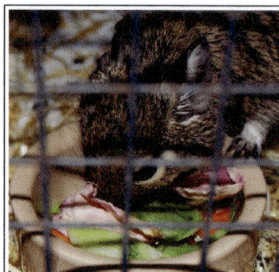

Giving each degu their own bowl to eat from is essential to avoid squabbles over food.

Degus are naturally inquisitive and will soon figure out where to get a drink from.

Toys

The variety of toys suitable for degus is quite extensive, which is good because degus need plenty of toys and objects to investigate inside their enclosure to keep their minds occupied. Degus are very smart and can get bored with toys after a while, so having a good selection that you can rotate regularly is a great way to keep them happy. Toys for degus need not be expensive, and in fact it's often the cheapest they find the most enjoyable. For example, stuffing a cardboard tube with a few treats and plenty of hay is a great way to keep them occupied. There are lots of suggestions for you to try on the enrichment page of Degutopia's website (link at the end of the chapter), but here are just a few:

Degus really love hammocks and they make a must-have addition to any cage!

(Image: Maria Quinn)

Rope toys are great for hanging in the cage, made from natural cotton or sisal.

Mesh cubes stuffed with shredded paper will make nest-building fun!

(Image: Alison Baxter)

Toys made from natural sisal or hemp are also great fun for your degus!

Acrylic bird or parrot toys are also good for degu mental stimulation.

Climbing branches are good for the teeth, too.

(Image: Melissa Tiley-Waters)

An important note about branches and wood:

Not all woods are safe for degus, in fact many types of wood have **toxic** properties and could be harmful for your degus if they chew them. Always stick to those wood types known to be degu-safe, which include:

Apple, Hazel, Kiln-dried pine and Hawthorn (thorns removed). *If in doubt, leave it out!*

Substrate

There is quite a wide variety of substrate types you can use to line the base of your degus' cage in order to keep it clean and hygienic. The type you decide to use for your degus depends on personal preference, but to help you to choose here is a list of the pro's and con's of some common types suitable for degu use:

Substrate	Example brands	Pro's	Con's
Kiln-dried pine shavings	-	*Anti-bacterial properties *Fairly absorbent *Retains smells well *Cheap *Can be composted	*Contains allergens some degus with wood-dust allergies are sensitive to *Light and easily kicked out of the cage *Can be tricky to clean out
Chopped straw	"Russel Bedding"	*Low-dust and hypoallergenic *Cheap *Can be composted	*Not very absorbent *Light and easily kicked out of the cage *Doesn't retain smells so well

Recycled paper/card	"Finacard" "Carefresh"	*Low-dust and hypoallergenic *Heavy and more likely to remain in the cage *Absorbent *Good for the environment *Can be composted	*Can be more expensive than other substrate
Processed wood pulp	"Megazorb"	*Low-dust and hypoallergenic *Absorbent *Retains smells well *Can buy fairly cheaply in bulk *Can be composted	*Light and easily kicked out of the cage *Usually can only be bought in bulk (horse bedding)
Shredded paper	-	*Low-dust and hypoallergenic *Cheap (usually free!) *Good for the environment *Can be composted	*Not very absorbent *Light and easily kicked out of the cage *Avoid using printed paper if your degus try to eat the paper regularly

Please note that cedar wood chips must not be used as degu substrate, as these are highly toxic when eaten. Wood-based cat litter pellets must also be avoided as they present a danger of intestinal impaction when eaten, and because they are hard are also bad for degu feet. Some degus are allergic to wood dusts, so substrate should be switched to a low-dust alternative if you notice any sneezing or wheezing in degus housed on shavings.

Cleaning

Degus are very clean animals and like their living space to be kept hygienic. Degus don't normally produce large quantities of urine and you will find that their cage needs cleaning out about once per week. This should involve throwing out all substrate and replacing it with clean material, washing down all surfaces, shelves, ladders, feed bowls and toys, and replacing their nesting material. Use only hot water and washing-up liquid suitable for sensitive skin to clean with, as degus can develop skin allergies to other cleaning products (even pet-safe disinfectants).

Check out the following related pages on Degutopia's website:

- Degu housing and environment:
    - http://www.degutopia.co.uk/deguhouse.htm
- Enrichment and toys for degus:
    - http://www.degutopia.co.uk/deguenrich.htm
- List of woods with toxic properties:
    - http://www.degutopia.co.uk/degutoxic.htm

Degu Diet

Hay you! Did you know that the absolute most important part of your degus' diet is hay? Don't be tempted to think that hay is boring for your degus to eat, or not as interesting as their brightly-packaged hard feed; degus *need* to eat hay, every day, to be healthy. Remember that wild degus eat mostly dried grasses and herbs? This means that their digestive system is specially designed for this kind of diet, and above all, degus really do love eating hay! Without enough fibre in their diet provided through eating hay, the degu gut can deteriorate, their molar teeth can overgrow, their general health can suffer, and they can develop behavioural problems. You may not have realised that hay was important for all those things in degu life!

Because hay is so important to degu health, it should form the majority of their diet. Hay should be provided freely to your degus, throughout the day, for them to browse on. Degus can extract most of the energy they need from hay. However, degus also need a few extra vitamins and minerals to be healthy, which aren't found in hay. This is what hard feed is needed for.

Hard Feed

This is the term given to the pellets or mixes that are available to buy from pet shops and supermarkets. Hard feed needs to be offered **restrictively**, because given the choice your degu would eat the high-energy hard feed over hay (much like offering a child the choice between vegetables and

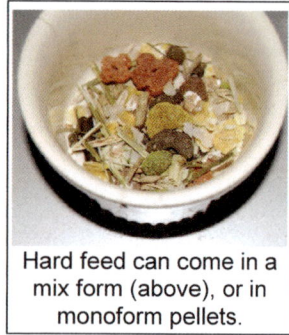

Hard feed can come in a mix form (above), or in monoform pellets.

sweets!). Over-eating hard feed can lead to several health problems, including obesity, intestinal degradation, and molar overgrowth. The recommended daily allowance of hard feed for an adult degu is **10 g per degu per day**; this can be measured out with a 25 ml shot glass (which should hold 10 g of most hard feeds). For juvenile degus less than 6 months old, this portion should be reduced to 5–8 g per degu (it can be increased to the adult portion once the degus reach 6 months old). The exact type or brand of hard feed you choose to give to your degus needs to be considered carefully. Try to opt for a degu-specific feed where possible, or one suitable for guinea pigs or chinchillas. However, you should *always* check the ingredients and nutrition list on the packet to make sure that the feed is suitable for degus.

Things to check:

Ingredients- Look out for any sugary substances such as glucose, honey, molasses, fructose or syrup. Degus cannot tolerate free sugars in the diet on a regular basis as they are prone to developing diabetes- they just aren't able to metabolise these sugars from their system quickly enough. Similarly, any feed containing dried fruit pieces should be avoided, as dried fruits are high in free sugars. It is also wise to check that there are no meat or animal derivatives included in the feed; degus are strictly herbivorous and cannot digest animal proteins.

Nutritional breakdown- This is a list of the balance of different nutritional components in the feed, stated in percentages. It is important to check this, because degus require a low-protein, low-fat, high-fibre diet. The following 'traffic-light' system can be used to check this:

GREEN- Good levels for degus	ORANGE- Moderate levels for degus	RED- Poor levels for degus
Protein = 15 % or less	Protein = 16-17 %	Protein = 18 % or more
Fat/oil = 4 % or less	Fat/oil = 5-6 %	Fat/oil = 7 % or more
Fibre = 15 % or more	Fibre = 10-14 %	Fibre = 9 % or less
Total sugars = less than 5 %		Total sugars = more than 5 %

Vitamin and mineral content will also be stated in the breakdown. These should include:

- **Vitamin A** (around 15,000-30,000 IU/kg)
- **Vitamin D$_3$** (around 1,000-1,500 IU/kg)
- **Vitamin C** (around 250 mg/kg)
- **Vitamin E** (around 50 mg/kg)
- **Copper** (around 10 mg/kg)

These vitamins are vital for healthy degus. It is known that some of these vitamins, like vitamin C, can be synthesised by the degu's body, but because they are so important for immune system health, dietary supplementation is beneficial.

A list of recommended hard feed brands that are commonly available and suitable for degu use can be found on the diet section of Degutopia's website (link at the end of the chapter).

Vegetable Supplementation

In addition to hay and hard feed, there is another key component of the degu diet. Fresh vegetable matter should be offered, sparingly, to your degus once or twice per week. Fresh vegetation is an important part of the diet, as it

Degus should be offered a small selection of fresh veg.

contains nutritional substances important to health that are difficult to include in hard feeds and cannot be synthesised by the body (e.g. essential amino acids). Degus typically require a selection of small (thumb-nail sized) pieces of vegetable matter on occasion, however not all degus enjoy all types of vegetable! The following table should help you to select the most appropriate vegetables for your degus.

Vegetable table

Vegetables that need to be fed in moderation to avoid bloating	Vegetables that are higher in free sugars and should only be given once per month (note that diabetic degus should not be given these)	Other vegetables that may be given weekly to degus
Cabbage (all types)	Peas	Butternut squash
Broccoli	Carrots	Pumpkin
Swede	Sweet potato (raw)	Marigold flowers
Green beans	Apple	Dried herbs (oregano; mint; parsley; basil; chives; comfrey; lemon balm; coriander)
Fresh grass	Cucumber	
Dandelion leaves	Cherry tomato	
Fresh herbs (oregano; mint; parsley; basil; chives; comfrey; lemon balm; coriander)	Sweetcorn/maize/corn-on-the-cob	Red pepper, green pepper
Carrot tops		Radish
Cauliflower (leaves and stalk)		Spring onion
Courgette		Dried rose petals
Leek		Rosehips
Asparagus		Beetroot
Celery		
Brussels sprouts		
Lettuce		

Vegetable matter, particularly green vegetation, requires moderating because it can cause bloating and even diarrhoea. Bloating is very uncomfortable for your degus! Offer veg sparingly, and if your degus turn their noses up at the fresh stuff, try offering some dried veggies instead!

Treats

Of course, all degu owners want to treat their degus from time to time with something a bit special. Treats are just that- foods that degus really enjoy, but that they should only get from time to time, or sparingly. Treats are also ideal for training work as a reward, which we'll talk about later. The following foods make perfect degu treats:

- **Sunflower/pumpkin seeds** (one or two per degu per day)
- **Peanuts (shelled/unshelled)** (one per degu per week)
- **Whole hazelnuts in the shell** (one per degu per month)
- **Natural puffed rice** (several per degu per day)
- **Dried herbs** (offer as a dietary supplement)
- **Dried vegetables** (a few pieces per degu per week)
- **Dried rosehips** (one per degu per week)
- **Porridge oats** (one small pinch per degu per day)
- **Dried pasta** (one piece per degu per week)
- **Dried hawthorn leaves** (one or two per degu per week)
- **Apple** (one small piece per degu per month)

Treats like dried pasta and hazelnuts in the shell are also great for your degus' teeth. Nuts and seeds should not be given to overweight degus due to their high fat and protein content. Also, remember that apple contains free sugars so must not be given in large quantity or more often than once monthly, and if your degu is diabetic, do not offer them this at all. One last thing- don't be tempted to give your degu human breakfast cereals as treats. These often contain added sugars and vitamins that aren't good for your degu. Always be sure to check the treats you are using don't contain any added ingredients like this.

Water

Although a healthy adult degu won't drink very much (on average around 17 ml per degu per day), water is an essential part of their 'diet'. Water is required by the degu's body for all sorts of vital functions, and they cannot extract all the water they need from their food. This is why fresh drinking water must be supplied for your degus at all times. Tap water is just fine for your degus- as long as it is safe for you to drink. You must **not** treat your degus' drinking water with anything, unless directed by your vet for medical purposes.

When to Feed Your Degus

While hay should be provided throughout the day, it's best to give your degus their daily hard feed portion at a set time of day. Sticking to a feeding routine makes your degus feel more at home, as they know what to expect and when. Because degus are generally most active during the mornings and evenings, it's best to feed them at these times. However, if you want to encourage your degus to go to bed early, then feed them in the morning only; this will give them an energy boost in the morning, rather than just before bed! You can either give your degus all their hard feed portion at once, or split it into two half-portions twice daily (it's really up to you).

Note that degus perform 'coprophagy', i.e. they will eat and re-digest faecal pellets (droppings). This is completely normal behaviour, it actually allows them to extract extra nutrition from their food the second time it passes through their digestive system. Although it might seem unpleasant to us, it's really important to degus. Degu pups will eat the droppings of their parents and other adults in order to help populate their gut with the bacteria needed to help break down fibrous plant matter. Now that's handy!

Check out the following related pages on Degutopia's website:

- ⋛ Degu diet and nutrition:
  - ⋛ http://www.degutopia.co.uk/degudiet.htm
- ⋛ The role of sugar in the degu's diet:
  - ⋛ http://www.degutopia.co.uk/degusugar.htm
- ⋛ Vegetable feeding guide:
  - ⋛ http://www.degutopia.co.uk/deguveg.htm

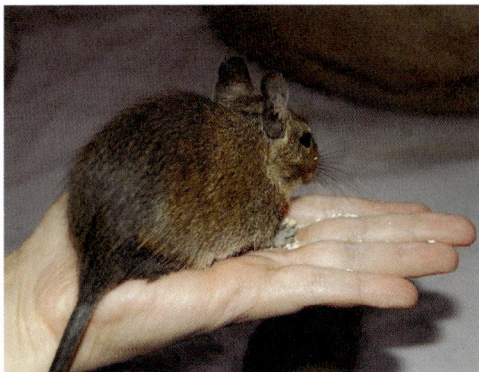

Training Your Degus

As you might have noticed by now, degus are very intelligent animals and are able to follow simple logic to perform certain tasks. Researchers have even found that degus can learn how to use 'tools' to achieve a reward (in that study degus actually worked out how to use a tiny rake to obtain a treat they couldn't reach!). This means that degus are very easy to train, which is extremely useful when taming and/or handling them. Because of their ability to shed their tail, degus need to be handled with care, and training is the best way to go about teaching them what you would like them to do. Degus that are very young or have just been given a brand new home may also be a little nervous at first, and training is by far the best way to encourage them to come out of their shells and begin to form a bond of trust with their new owner.

Training a degu is much the same as training any animal, from a horse to a dog, and is in fact very easy! Before you get started, there are a few golden rules that you should try to follow in order to succeed.

The Golden Rules of Training

- Training is all about developing trust between the trainer (you) and the trainee (degu).

- You must always ask your degu, rather than force them to do something, for training to work. Allowing them to think they have a choice about what to do is essential!

- The learning process is based on a system of positive and negative feedback resulting from your degu's actions.

- Positive feedback is given to your degus in the form of rewards.

- Rewards are positive things that the degu is motivated to work for.

- Rewards greatly increase the rate at which your degu learns a new task.

- Rewards are mentally ranked by the degu- the higher the degu values the reward, the more motivated your degu will be to work for it.

- An example of a highly valued reward is food, this is the best training aid you have.

- Good foods to use when training are: your degu's daily feed broken into little bits, natural puffed rice, flaked corn/maize or flaked peas (available from some pet shops, break them into little bits), crumbs of wholemeal bread and natural, rolled (porridge) oats.

- To maintain your degu's attention, always use small bits of food.

- Make sure you don't over-feed your degu during training, as this can lead to obesity.

- Food is not the only training aid- many degus appreciate a belly rub just as much!

- Talk to your degu in a soothing voice throughout training, as this will encourage them and get them used to how you sound.

- Always reward your degu's actions- a continuous reward system is proven to facilitate learning more than an intermittent or random schedule.

- Be patient! Training takes time, and remember that all degus learn at different rates.

- One last point to make is that although young degus can be easier to train, and pick things up much faster, older degus can be trained too (you CAN teach an old degu new tricks!!).

Before you start any training work with young or new degus, it's important to consider that they need some time to settle in to their new home, first. It's advisable to put your degu cage in a quiet room during the first week or so you have them, so that they get used to all the new sounds, smells, routines, and people in their new home. Try to avoid handling them or disturbing them too much during this period. Once they seem happy to be out and about in the cage while you're around, it's time to start some training work!

Perhaps one of the best things to start training or taming your degus with is 'hand training', i.e. asking your degu to climb onto your hands when offered out to them. This is ideal, as it not only encourages your degu to put their trust in you, it will also come in very handy for getting your degus in and out of the cage! You can start this training either while your degus are inside their cage (door open, of course!), or, if they're comfortable and relaxed, in their play area. Here's how to do it:

1. Ensure your degus are relaxed, happy, and curious about what's going on. Ideally, they should be happy to come up to you for a treat. If they aren't yet comfortable with this, don't rush on, simply take your time building up their confidence every day by offering them a suitable treat.

2. To start with, offer your degus a couple of treats for approaching your hands, so that they form a 'positive association'. Receiving a treat reinforces what your degu is learning as they go along, making them remember what you have taught them!

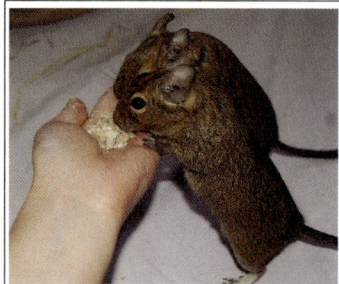

Encourage your degus to put both forepaws on your hand for a reward.

3. Now try holding out your palm, face up, and using your other hand, offer them a treat so that they need to put one or both of their forepaws onto your palm to get to it. As soon as the degu does this, release the treat.

4. Repeat this step several times until the degu has got the hang of it- repetition is really important for the degu to learn the task properly. If you're not sure the degu is doing it right, don't be afraid to go back one stage and start again before moving on.

5. Next, hold the treat a little further back, so that the degu has to lean over your palm to get at it. What you're doing here is working up to asking your degu to stand on your hand for the treat, but this is a big step for them so it's really important to build up to this slowly. At this point you should only be giving out a treat when your degu leans over, and not for when they just put a paw on your palm. This will

encourage them to try that bit harder for their reward and to move the training along.

6.   When you think your degu is ready, you can try asking them to put both forepaws and their hind feet onto your hand. At first, the degu may be a little reluctant, because this is a big step for them- they need to trust that you're not suddenly going to do something unexpected! When they stand on your hand for the first time, remember to keep very still and always allow your degu to jump off when they choose to- choice is the key to successful training work!

7.   Congratulations! Your degu has now shown that they are learning to trust you, hurray! But the training doesn't end here, you'll need to repeatedly ask your degus to get onto your hand in this way as often as you can, every day, in order for them to get better at it. Eventually, you will be able to simply present your palm in front of your degu, and they will jump on- whether they get a treat or not!

Remember that this training is by far the best way to handle your degu. You should **never, ever** use your hands to corner your degu, or try to grab them. By doing this you are acting like a predator in the eyes of your degu, and by forcing them to do something they aren't sure about, or can get away from, you will be stressing them and breaking any trust they have built up in you so far. *So don't do it*! There are alternative methods for getting your degu into and out of the cage, which you can learn by visiting the 'tube training' and 'vocal commands' sections of Degutopia's site (links at the end of the chapter).

When training, it's worth remembering the four R's:

Routine, Repetition, Reward and Relaaaaax!

(Your degu can easily pick up on any stress or tension you might be feeling!).

Check out the following related pages on Degutopia's website:

- Degu training:
    - http://www.degutopia.co.uk/degutrain.htm
- Steps for hand training your degus:
    - http://www.degutopia.co.uk/degutrainhand.htm
- Steps for tube training your degus:
    - http://www.degutopia.co.uk/degutraintube.htm
- Tips for using voice commands:
    - http://www.degutopia.co.uk/degutrainvoice.htm
- Extra help with training/taming a nervous degu:
    - http://www.degutopia.co.uk/degutame.htm

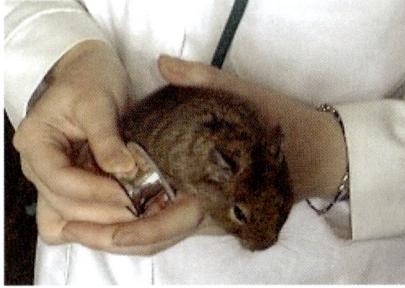

Keeping Your Degus Healthy

Every owner wants their degus to be happy and in top health, and there are a few simple checks you can do regularly to ensure your pets are in their prime!

Weight

One of the best indicators of a degu's health is their weight. Because degus are good at hiding problems (in the wild, this would help stop them being selected by a predator), keeping an eye on their weight is important as it may be the first clue that something isn't right. An adult degu (over 1 year old) should weigh in the **healthy range of 220–250 g**. A non-pregnant degu weighing more than 250 g is overweight, which affects their health as it puts them at an increased risk of

Weighing your degus regularly is a great way to keep an eye on their health.

developing kidney, liver and heart problems, as well as increasing the risk of diabetes. If your degus is overweight, try increasing the amount of exercise they get, cut back on the hard feed portion of their diet slightly (but not on hay!), and reduce the quantity of treats, particularly those high in protein and fats. An adult degu weighing less than 220 g is underweight, which is often an indicator of an underlying health problem. If your degu is underweight, it's a good idea to give them a check-up with your vet, particularly to make sure their molar teeth are in good order. It's recommended that you weigh your degus once a month, and keep a record of their weight each time. To do this, you can use flat-topped kitchen scales, with a few porridge oats sprinkled on top. Your degu should be happy to sit there and eat the oats, while you read off their weight.

Water

Monitoring your degus' drinking behaviour is particularly important, because of the link with diabetes. A pair of healthy, adult degus will get through about 1000 ml of water per month, although note that this will vary according to season, temperature and activity level. A diabetic degu will drink far more than this each month, and also produce much more urine. You should therefore watch out for these signs that could suggest one or more of your degus may be diabetic, in which case your vet will be able to test them and advise further.

Coat

Your degus' coat condition is often also a good indicator of general health. A healthy degu will have a glossy coat that covers their entire body, and does not have any bald patches. To keep your degus' coat in good condition, allow them access to a dust bath every day, and you can also add a few drops of evening primrose oil to their feed once per month. Note that degus do shed their coats twice each year (in the spring and again in autumn), during which time you might notice 'stripes' appearing in their fur, and a lot more loose hair about the cage. While it is normal for degus to shed their fur, they should never develop bald patches at any point.

Behaviour

Another excellent indicator of general health in the degu is their behaviour. A healthy degu should be alert, attentive and inquisitive, showing an interest in you and their surroundings. Ill degus will often become 'lethargic', where they sleep much more than normal, sit in one place with their fur ruffled up, and refuse to move or interact with other degus or their surroundings. A lethargic degu should always be examined by a vet right away, as there could be a serious problem needing urgent attention.

Eyes

Check that your degus' eyes are clear, fully open, and free of any discharge. Eyelids that have become stuck shut, or eyes that produce watery or opaque discharge, are indicative of an eye infection (discussed in the next chapter). Eyes that appear otherwise normal, but have a small circle of blue-grey at the centre, represent cataracts. We'll also discuss cataracts in the illness chapter.

Nose

The degu nose should also be clean, dry, and free from any discharge or crusting, and there should be no signs of wetness around the mouth. Runny noses can indicate an allergy, a respiratory infection, or teeth problems, so be sure to get these signs checked out by your vet.

Feet

Undersides of all four of your degus' feet should be checked regularly, to examine for any signs of bumblefoot (see next chapter). The skin over the pads should appear healthy and smooth, with no signs of sores, ulcers/blisters, or any weeping, redness or discharge.

Teeth

Keep an eye on your degus' incisor teeth. The front surface of each tooth should be a bright orange colour in the adult degu; if the teeth appear pale or creamy-white this can be linked with underlying illness or nutritive deficiencies. The incisors should not be too long and should be worn down evenly. Overgrown incisors can indicate molar teeth problems and need further investigation by your vet (see next chapter).

Check out the following related pages on Degutopia's website:

⋧ Degu health and degu 'fit club':

⋧ http://www.degutopia.co.uk/deguhealth.htm

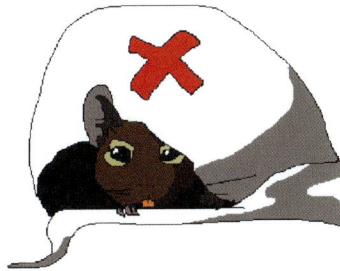

Common Degu Illnesses

Although all owners of course hope their degus will never get ill, it always pays to be prepared and to know what signs to look for. Remember that degus live for a fairly long time, so there is a chance that at some point in their lifetime they will need to see a vet, even if it's only for a check-up. Because degus are still considered a fairly 'exotic' animal, it's well worth contacting all the local vets in your area to find one that has experience with the species. This will save time if your degus ever need to visit the vet in an emergency. The rest of this chapter is dedicated to the **most common** degu illnesses, how to identify them, and the treatment needed.

 Note that this chapter is a guide only; you should **always seek veterinary attention** whenever you suspect your degus might be ill.

Additional examples can be found in the illness section of Degutopia's website (link at the end of the chapter).

Molar/Incisor Teeth Problems

This is the first illness on the list, because it is **by far the most common**. Over 60 % of degus seen by a vet have problems caused by, or relating to, teeth conditions. The reason teeth problems are so prevalent in degus is partly due to the nature of their teeth, which continually grow, and partly due to their dietary requirements. We discussed before how important hay is in the degu's diet, and how important it is for their health. Degus *need* to eat hay on a regular basis to maintain the wear of their molar teeth. Without it, the molars can overgrow, causing painful, sharp points (spurs) to develop, which lacerate the tongue and cheeks. This makes eating anything extremely difficult for the degu. Secondary complications can then develop, including overgrowth of the incisor teeth.

Overgrowth of the incisor teeth usually occurs secondary to molar problems.

(Image: Ellen Bown)

Signs and symptoms

Weight loss; pawing at the mouth; difficulty eating/food dropping from the mouth; loss of appetite; wetness around the mouth; overgrowth of the incisors.

Treatment

Your vet will need to examine the molar teeth as soon as possible under general anaesthesia, and file down any sharp edges. Long incisors should be burred down at the same time. Dietary modification my be needed.

Prevention

By far the best prevention is to ensure your degus are getting the correct diet, and eating plenty of hay every day. If your degus aren't eating their hay, you can try cutting back on their hard feed and treats, and adding some dried herbs to some good quality hay.

Diabetes

Another extremely common disorder of the degu is diabetes. Degus are unable to metabolise dietary sugar in the usual way, so as a result, high levels of sugar in the diet cause the degu to develop diabetes. This disease is characterised by very high levels of glucose in the blood, with excess glucose excreted in the urine. This puts a much larger strain on the kidneys over time, and can lead to other kidney-related disorders.

Signs and symptoms

Drinking behaviour increases dramatically; large volumes of urine produced; cataracts develop in both eyes (see following); Other degus may lick affected degu's urine (it will be sweet).

Treatment

The most important part of the treatment is to immediately cut out any foods in the degu's diet that contain any free sugars. This includes fruit, and any veg with a higher sugar content. Unfortunately, there is no 'cure' for diabetes once developed, so the condition must be managed with an appropriate diet, and regular urinary glucose testing.

Prevention

As you have probably guessed by now, prevention of diabetes largely relies on restricting all sugar-containing foods in the degu diet. Although degus can have some free sugar foods in small quantity (such as apple), these should be offered in moderation and infrequently.

Cataracts

This is the term given to the clouding/opacity in the lens of the eye. Cataracts are also fairly common in the degu, because of their link with diabetes. Diabetes causes a build up of sorbitol in the eye lens, making it become opaque- this can greatly reduce the degu's vision. However, cataracts are not always linked to diabetes in the degu, as they can also inherit a genetic condition that causes cataracts to form. This is most easy to identify in degus that only

Cataracts appear as small, grey disks in the centre of the eye.

(Image: Phil Noce)

have a cataract in one eye; diabetes-related cataracts *always* affect both eyes. Degus with bilateral cataracts (both eyes) will learn to rely more on smell and other senses to get about.

Signs and symptoms

A small patch of opaque clouding in the centre of the eye (one or both eyes); this may become more obvious as the cataract develops further. Advanced cataracts may noticeably affect the vision (bumping into objects, reluctant to run around unfamiliar areas).

Treatment

As with diabetes, there is no 'cure' for cataracts, they may only be managed. If cataracts are diabetes-related, treat as for diabetes. In addition it can be beneficial to help the degu compensate for reduced vision, such as by keeping cage layout the same so they can get around from memory, and using essential oils in the play area (e.g. at the cage exit, near the dust bath, etc.) for them to navigate by scent.

Prevention

For diabetes-related cataracts, prevention is the same as for diabetes. For genetically inherited cataracts, prevention is purely achieved through not breeding from affected degus.

Tail De-gloving

As mentioned before, degus are able to shed their tail as an anti-predatory defence mechanism, so a common injury in degus occurs through accidental shedding of the tail. This may suddenly happen if a degu is restrained by their tail, gets their tail caught in something, or is bitten badly on the tail by a cagemate. Although it's not pleasant to see, the process seems to be painless for the degu and heals rapidly. Once de-gloved, the tail will not grow back and the degu will be left with a stump, however they do learn to compensate eventually for balance.

Signs and symptoms

A de-gloved tail will leave the affected part of the tail's tendons and vertebrae exposed, there will be some bleeding of the area. A sheath of skin and hair will be torn away completely.

Treatment

Bleeding should stop within 20 minutes and the exposed tendons begin to dry out. This process will continue for a few days until the dried-out end is chewed off, leaving a stump. If bleeding continues, or any swelling or discharge is seen in the tail end, seek veterinary attention.

Prevention

Don't handle or restrain a degu by their tail, even in an emergency! Also ensure that wheels are spoke-free and can't trap tails while in use.

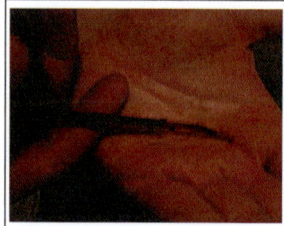

Tail de-gloving exposes the tendons and vertebrae (Image: Mike Smith)

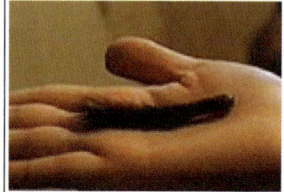

leaving behind a sheath of skin and hair.

The tail stump will not grow back.

Bumblefoot

This condition of the sole of the foot is also known as 'pododermatitis' and is caused by pressure sores, as a result of standing/walking regularly on rough or uneven surfaces, particularly wire mesh floors. Bumblefoot is also very common in chinchillas and guinea pigs, close relatives of the degu. It is very painful for the animal, and can often cause them to chew at their feet causing further damage. Luckily it is preventable and needn't be a common problem for captive degus.

Signs and symptoms

Degu is reluctant to walk about normally, often limping or becoming inactive; soles of the feet appear to have ulcers or open sores; weeping or lacerated areas on the pads of the feet (hind or forepaws); repeated chewing or self-mutilation of the feet.

Treatment

Firstly all mesh surfaces or uneven/rough surfaces inside the cage must be covered or removed- including checking the running wheel. Padding to shelves may be provided in the form of towels, reed mats or fleece- these must be replaced/washed regularly to help prevent infection in any wounds on the feet. Wounds and sores must receive veterinary attention and possibly antibiotic medication. Bathe all wounds twice daily in a saline solution to help prevent infection and speed healing.

Prevention

Prevention of bumblefoot is a must wherever possible, so be sure to check that any exposed mesh inside your degus' cage is covered or replaced with a solid surface. Never use a cage with a mesh base. Mesh shelves can be covered with ceramic tiles or replaced with kiln-dried pine planks. Avoid using any substrate that causes an uneven surface, such as wood pellets or gravel.

Infections

Infections in the degu can be another common disorder and occur in a variety of forms. Unfortunately, some infections are internal and don't have any obvious outward signs; these are the hardest to treat as degus often hide the fact they might be feeling unwell, until they become very poorly and weak- this is a very good reason to weigh your degus regularly to keep an eye on their general health, and to get them checked out by your vet as soon as they show any change in their behaviour.

Abscesses typically occur when an old injury or bite wound becomes infected, other infections can occur unexpectedly through contamination from the general environment- remember that bacteria are found everywhere, even in the cleanest of cages!

Signs and symptoms

Abscess- one or more soft lumps appear on the degu's body; there may be some pussy discharge. Eye infection- creamy or brownish discharge around the eye, especially during grooming; eyelid sticks shut; discharge from/around eye. Ear infection- repeated scratching at/inside ear; pungent smell from ear; head tilting to one side; degu may be disorientated and lethargic. Respiratory infection- sneezing/wheezing; may be discharge from nose; may be lethargic. Gastrointestinal infection- loss of appetite; diarrhoea; weight loss; lethargy.

Treatment

Veterinary attention must be sought immediately as antibiotics are essential for treating and clearing the infection. The type of antibiotic needed will be specific to the type of infection; more details about recommended antibiotics for degus can be found on the veterinary medications page of Degutopia's site (link at the end of the chapter).

Prevention

Good cage hygiene is important, although infections can occur even in the cleanest of environments. Be vigilant, and clean any wounds immediately with saline solution, twice daily, to help prevent infection.

Check out the following related pages on Degutopia's website:

- Additional degu illnesses:
    - http://www.degutopia.co.uk/deguill.htm
- Degu veterinary medications guide:
    - http://www.degutopia.co.uk/deguvetlist.htm

Quick Reference

Degu age: pup	**Less than 6 weeks**
Degu age: juvenile	**6 weeks – less than 1 year**
Degu age: adult	**1 year or more**
Healthy adult weight	**220–250 g**
Recommended daily hard feed portion (6 months - adult)	**10 g per degu**
Recommended daily hard feed portion (juvenile – 6 months)	**5–8 g per degu**
Average adult water consumption (daily)	**17 ml per degu**
Average adult water consumption (monthly)	**1000 ml for 2 degus**
Recommended degu environmental temperature range	**18–22 °C**
Maximum temperature range limits for keeping degus	**15–25 °C**
Average age of puberty (male degus)	**12 weeks**

Average age of puberty (female degus)	**7 weeks**
Recommended minimum enclosure size for 2 adult degus	**W 45 x L 70 x H 100 cm**
Recommended daily exercise time outside the cage	**30 minutes +**
Maximum bar spacing	**2 cm**
Minimum running wheel diameter	**12 inches**
Degu-safe woods	**Apple, hazel, kiln-dried pine, hawthorn**

Index

17823214R00040

Printed in Poland
by Amazon Fulfillment
Poland Sp. z o.o., Wrocław